FIND YOUR POWER

RUNES

An Hachette UK Company
www.hachette.co.uk

First published in Great Britain in 2023 by Godsfield,
an imprint of Octopus Publishing Group Ltd
Carmelite House, 50 Victoria Embankment, London EC4Y 0DZ
www.octopusbooks.co.uk

ISBN 978-1-8418-1540-4

A CIP catalogue record for this book is available from the British Library

Printed and bound in China

10 9 8 7 6 5 4 3 2 1

Publisher: Lucy Pessell
Designer: Isobel Platt
Senior Editor: Hannah Coughlin
Assistant Editor: Samina Rahman
Production Controller: Allison Gonsalves
Illustrations: p. 8, 24, 52, 80, 110 created by Miroslava from the Noun Project

The translations in this book are from Bruce Dickins' 1915 *Runic and Heroic Poems of
the Old Teutonic Peoples*. Many other translations are available, and they are printed
here to simply give a flavour of the world we are hoping to step into.

FIND YOUR POWER

RUNES

KITTY GUILSBOROUGH

GODSFIELD

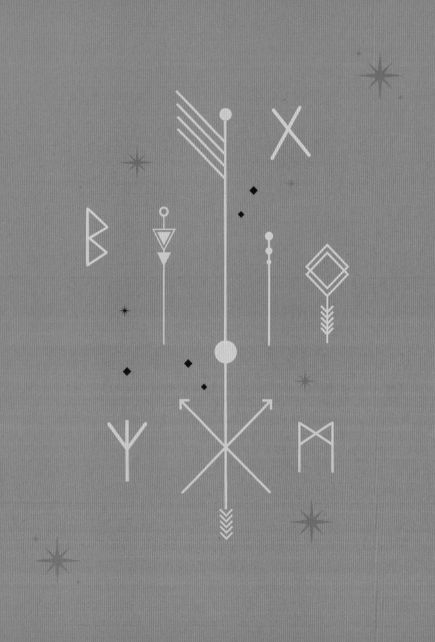

CONTENTS

FIND
YOUR
POWER

When daily life becomes busy and your time and energy is pulled in many different directions, it can be difficult to find time to nourish yourself. Prioritizing your own wellbeing can be a struggle and you risk feeling overwhelmed, unsure of where to turn and what you need in order to feel lighter and find your inner strength.

Taking some time to focus on yourself, answering questions you may be avoiding or facing problems that are simmering away under the surface is the best gift you can give yourself. But it can be difficult to know where to start.

Sometimes all you need to learn life's big lessons is a little guidance. In this series of books you will learn about personal healing, self empowerment and how to nourish your spirit. Explore practices which will help you to get clear on what you really want, and that will encourage you to acknowledge – and deal with – any limiting beliefs or negative thoughts that might be holding you back to living life to your fullest power.

These pocket-sized books provide invaluable advice on how to create the best conditions for a healthier, happier, and more fulfilled life Bursting with essential background, revealing insights and useful activities and exercises to enable yourself to understand and expand your personal practices every day, it's time to delve into your spiritual journey and truly Find Your Power.

Other titles in the series:

- *Find Your Power: Manifest*
- *Find Your Power: Tarot*
- *Find Your Power: Numerology*

INTRODUCTION

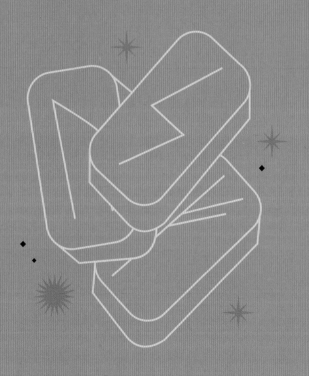

The word "rune" has many meanings. A *friend* in Icelandic, a *whisper* in Old English, a *secret* in Old Irish. In Finnish and Welsh it's a *song*, a *chant* or a *charm*. In Old Norse, where it all began, it's a *mystery*.

Runes are all these things, and they are also an alphabet for a language no living person has ever heard spoken as a native tongue: the last people who wrote this language for their everyday ways lived in the eighth century. This is the sacred language of people who lived almost two thousand years ago. The language, in many ways, of our predecessors on this Earth.

Whether or not our ancestors were *literally* rune-writers, the world we live in is directly shaped by theirs. We are the inheritors of their language (if we speak English); and we venerate their gods as (super) heroes. Our working weeks follow the pattern of their holy days

– Moon's Day, Tiw's Day, Wotan's Day et cetera – and our world trade follows the pattern of their shipping. A double rune adorns all modern technology as the symbol for Bluetooth: ᚼ + ᛒ, Hagall from the Younger Futhark (see below) and Berkana (page 91) combined into one singular bindrune (two merged runes) that has come to signify an invisible, intangible communication.

They left us their world, and their words.

So let us listen.

Runes, as noted, are an alphabet. Three alphabets, in fact: the Elder Futhark, the Younger Futhark and the Anglo-Saxon Futhorc. Much as our own word "alphabet" derives from "alpha" + "beta", the word "futhark" comes from the first seven letters of the runic alphabet: **F**ehu, **U**ruz, **Th**urisaz, **A**nsuz, **R**aido, **K**enaz.

There are 24 runes of the Elder Futhark, divided into three Ættir. An Ætt is a family, and each family of eight runes belong to an ancient Norse mythological figure. Freja, the goddess of love, rules the first eight. Heimdall, the watcher at heaven's doors, rules the second. The third belongs to Tyr, the mysterious self-sacrificing god from the beginning of time itself. The origins of these Ættir are lost to time, and so are many of the stories of each mythological figure that watches over them – and yet from what remains, we can see that each Ætt is a complete journey in and of itself.

While these words may seem alien and off-putting to you now, by the end of this book they (and the 17 other runic letters) will feel like friends. This may seem silly – how could a letter be a friend? – however these symbols have ancient resonance. Each one carries with it a name; a literal translation of that name; and a

deep symbolic meaning. Often, each rune carries an accompanying poem or riddle. The rune is the answer to the riddle; and the riddle is the song of the rune.

This is less complicated than it sounds: think of how the letter A has come to signify something done well, an F signifies a failure and X symbolizes simultaneously mystery, treasure or even Jesus Christ. We use letters as symbols all the time. It's just that the runic alphabet takes it one step further.

These meanings, then, are what allow us to use the runes for divination. This, of course, is why you're reading this book in the first place: we are not scholars, we are not historians, even if – like them – we are here to figure stuff out.

Runes, in the sense we mean, are a collection of 24 engraved stones (occasionally bones, sometimes painted cards). Each stone, bone or card carries on it one rune. We take three of these at random (sometimes fewer, sometimes more) and we use those three runes to tell a story or answer a question.

You will notice that some runes have an additional reversed interpretation. If you draw a reversed stone, it can help to understand its message if you read about what each position could mean. Not all runes have an upright an reversed, and the meanings often intertwine as two sides of a coin.

We bring ourselves to the stones, and the stones offer up a new perspective on our lives. The ancient words, translated from Icelandic or Anglo-Saxon, give us

We bring ourselves to the stones, and the stones offer up a new perspective on our lives.

> **What we take from the stones is what we put in: like all magic and all spirituality, you have to give in order to get.**

new ways of looking at a problem. They are prompts for where we might go next. They are story-starters, inspiration-givers, light-bringers.

The runes become a friend in dark times; the song of your life, with chorus and verses; the persistent chant of something you already know to be true. You see, the art of telling runes is the art of listening to your own subconscious: the secrets of the self, the whispers you've maybe tried to ignore. After all, when you can buy magic from Amazon, you have to understand that at least some of that magic is coming directly from *you*. This isn't to say that overnight you've become a witch, a psychic or a fortune teller: it's just to say that you are the expert in your own life. Sometimes, when we talk about things like Tarot cards or runestones, it's easy to fall into the trap of believing that they tell *us* what to do. It's easy to think that they are revealing a future that's already there, and already set. You are the only person who can tell your story, and the only person who can change it. Your life is your own.

What we take from the stones is what we put in: like all magic and all spirituality, you have to give in order to get. Bring your question sincerely to the stones. Bring your story with you to the meaning. And find the answers you most need.

The runic alphabet is an ancient system that has been used (and abused) by many groups over the centuries. The difficult history of the association of runes with far-right groups, such as the Nazis and Neo-Nazis, cannot be ignored – but nor can this history be allowed to become the only history of runes. Rune-telling, like so many spiritual practices, traditionally belongs to the outsiders: to a diverse, beautiful collection of storytellers from all kinds of backgrounds and worlds. We must, as rune-scholars, reject all claim that these stories belong to those who seek to divide us. These stories belong to all who live in the world that the ancients shaped: thus, they belong to everyone. When we tell runes, we do so in the knowledge that we must use their powerful history and strength for good.

CHOOSING
YOUR RUNES

So what now? Where do runes come from?

You can make or buy your first set for not much money. Don't feel you need to go all out here: when you're beginning, it might take a little while to figure out the kind of runes you like. Most of us go through several sets before we settle on the runes that feel right in our hands. Make or buy something that is absolutely accessible to you; give yourself time to find out what kind of rune-reader you are. Give yourself grace.

Whether or not you make your own, it's a great idea to write out the alphabet as we learn each symbol. You could take a journal with space for each rune, or just draw each one onto a Post-it Note.

When I first learned, I wrote out a notecard for each rune – just as if I were studying at school. I wanted to take the runes seriously, just

as I wanted the runes to take my life seriously. By taking the time to learn, I was also taking the time for myself.

It familiarizes us with the shape, but it also gives us a certain ownership over the symbol: this is my handwriting, this is how I write this rune. The act of writing is incredibly powerful. Writing has been proven to help us process bad feelings, like loss, and reassert good feelings, like gratitude. It also helps us learn with different parts of our brain, rather than just the purely academic: what the hand does, the mind remembers.

As I did, you can surround each symbol with ideas: meaningful words and phrases, snippets of the traditional poems, or things it calls to mind from your own experiences. When we relate a rune back to the things we already know, we give it life.

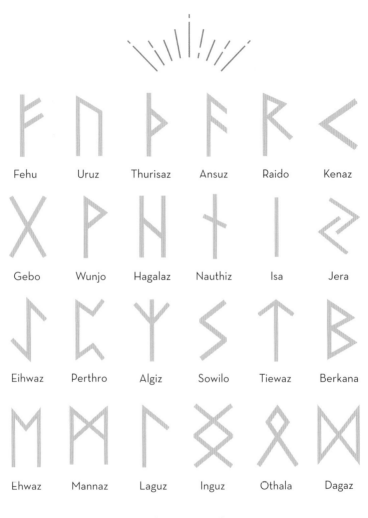

Fehu	Uruz	Thurisaz	Ansuz	Raido	Kenaz
Gebo	Wunjo	Hagalaz	Nauthiz	Isa	Jera
Eihwaz	Perthro	Algiz	Sowilo	Tiewaz	Berkana
Ehwaz	Mannaz	Laguz	Inguz	Othala	Dagaz

You imbue the symbols with your energy as you write, draw, carve or paint the runes – and this goes both for making and studying.

Creating your own set of runes is, obviously, an amazing way to get to know the Futhark – and to make each one unique to you. (It's also completely unnecessary if you feel like this is suddenly feeling daunting.)

If it appeals, however, much the easiest way is to do this with air-dry clay: form 24 tile shapes, emboss the rune into each one and let dry. You can also form the 24 tiles, let dry and paint the symbols onto each one. Some people carve; some people polish – but if you're capable of that, you're probably significantly beyond my guidance!

✳

When we relate a rune back to the things we already know, we give it life.

✳

To work with
something
beautiful is a
gift; to take a
little space and
time to sit with a
beautiful object
is healing in and
of itself.

Here's the thing: it is completely possible, very easy and absolutely fine to just buy yourself a set of runestones. Many people who tell the runes will purchase a set, either at a magick-type "occult" shop, or even (whisper it) online. There are so many beautiful sets of runestones available and made of all kinds of materials: not just stone but carved bone, shaped clay, even antler.

Gemstones are the most common, and you can choose your gemstone by the quality you most hope to

bring to your work: of course, many gemstones are financially out of reach for us, but semi-precious stones have a great deal of spiritual power. Amethyst brings clarity and calm, for example; jade for prosperity; jasper for consolation.

It's you, and your energy, that power the stories your stones tell you.

And if the thought of crystals having meaning brings you out in hives, please don't worry. Crystal magic is not for everyone, and maybe you just think the stones are beautiful. And that, too, is immensely powerful. To work with something beautiful is a gift; to take a little space and time to sit with a beautiful object is healing in and of itself.

Remember, it is you who imbues these stones with their magic: it's you, and your energy, that power the stories your stones tell you.

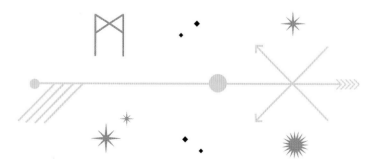

MAKING SPACE
FOR THE
OLD WAYS

We come to the runes, for the most part, to understand where to go; but when we come to the runes, we are drawing on our shared past. To discover the future we must be at one with our present; to be at one with our present, we must embrace the past.

We must welcome those old ways in and make space for them in our busy lives.

The Futhark comes from a time both simpler and much more complex than our own. Daily life was interwoven with wild mythology: the gods were as real to these people as their cattle, a horse and a hailstorm as magical as the beginning and end of the universe. A birch tree can be at once a source of life, and a source of spiritual succour in her guise as a goddess. The physical needs of man are on an equal footing with the winter's ice and a game of dice.

Each of these things – a storm, a goddess, a horse, a game – is just as likely to come out of the bag as any other. Life is made up of all these things: the big, the small, the beautiful, the terrifying.

And we know that, of course. Deep down, we know that. But it gets lost sometimes, under the weight of everything else. We can forget the spiritual in the endless, tedious, practical grind; but equally, we can take the ordinary things for granted while we reach fruitlessly for something more.

In our increasingly commercial society, we somehow distance ourselves from both the smallest and the biggest things in life. We find it hard to connect with our spiritual centres, but we also don't nourish those fundamental human things: we mostly don't toil the earth, or fear the coming winter, or know our place in nature.

And we try, too, to believe that death is not part of life. We try to believe that we are different to those who came before us: we try to believe that if we eat right and strive right and work right, we can escape fate in all things.

We can find ourselves, I suppose, a little adrift.

And so at this moment, before we begin our course of study, let's take some time.

Light a candle, if you can, and take a moment to breathe. Breathe

deep, and connect with your surroundings. Notice the room in which you sit; the land on which it is built. Picture the land long ago, before there was a city there, a town there, a village there. Picture the earth beneath you, and the roots and bones that live within it. Picture the life, and the death, all around you. Know you belong to it. Know it belongs to you, and with that belonging is your duty of care, and the earth's duty of care for you. Breathe deep: in through the nose, and out through the mouth. Feel the air in your mouth and throat and lungs. Be thankful; be open.

Soften your gaze and keep the flame in your gentle sight; and take the runes in your hand. Thank the fire for the light, and the stones for their cool weight. Feel your presence, and their presence. Breathe, and begin.

✳

To discover the future, we must be at one with our present; to be at one with our present, we must embrace the past.

✳

INTRODUCTION TO FREJA

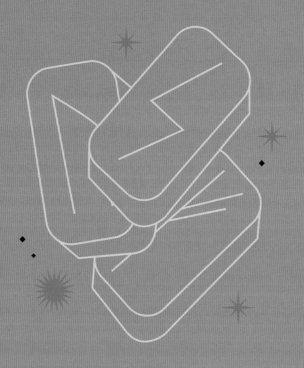

The first Ætt is that of Freja, the goddess of love and fertility. This Ætt is the home of the mother, the farmer, the torchlight, the gifts and the joy; the herdsman and horse; the breath in the lungs and the drizzle. It is the realm of life: the things that concerned the first men and should concern us today. It is real, tangible things: things of the physical plane above all else.

This Ætt is a lifecycle, from the seed in the hand, to the planting and germination to the harvest and sale and the profit, returned to the soil as more seeds. Is that all there is? That's all there ever is, if we're lucky. That's the greatest life a person can have: to learn, grow, return to the earth. We are one with the world, and the world is one with us. This is Freja's realm: the realm of the real, the true, the here and now. We're here for the Raido, the journey, and the trust we must feel for that which we control and that which controls us. This is a family of trust, and of balance: of trying to find the balance, always, in a world that's too big for us.

The drizzle, the thorn and the old wound that won't heal: these are the trials of Freja's Ætt. It is important, I think, to not dismiss these struggles. They are the struggles of real life, not the struggles of philosophy or what comes after. They are nothing grand, but they are not small, either. They matter; they must be heard, and each teaches us strengths and each comes with joys. The drizzle means sweet rain, which is not ice; the thorn is not a sword, nor an axe, but the prick of a plant that is living and strong. The old scars are teachers; the husband a protector, a warrior, a lover. These things are in all of us; this balance between the good and the bad something we strive for every day.

And after all this balance and striving, like a good mother, Freja leaves us in sunlight: of Gebo which is giving, and Wunjo which is joy.

WELCOMING
FREJA

There are two kinds of god, in the old Norse pantheons: gods of the Earth and gods of power.

Freja is a goddess who is tied to the Earth, and the things of the Earth: she exudes sex and femininity and fertility. She is a goddess in the true old sense: a Venus-esque, statuesque, hourglass goddess, who keeps the meadows of the dead. When she rides to battle she chooses her dead charm, and sends the rest to Valhalla, the Viking heaven-hall – but she chooses first. She may keep half the warriors, and all noble women; she feeds them well, with warmth and love and charm.

She is light and beauty, love and lust and babies and bodies, pretty things, fruit and flowers and firelight and candlelight and the Moon. She has the feathers of a falcon, and a chariot pulled by cats: she is surrounded by soft things that are fierce, and fierce things that are soft. She has the ferocious nature of the wild boar, but she is also throwing the dinner party where the boar turns on the spit. She nurses her young, and will kill to defend them. She will sacrifice to keep the home fires burning, if she has to, but she's happiest merely living. But there's nothing mere about it. Freja's world is a whole world, and frankly, what's life without these things? Men don't fight without having something to fight for, and men have fought for Freja. Anyone would fight for Freja.

For Freja is the sacred feminine. Sex and beauty are her weapons, and she wields them with abundance; she has no shame in her sexuality, no false modesty. She is beautiful, and she knows it. She loves sex, and pleasure, and her body. She is the Giver; the Brightener; the Lady.

Worship her with honey and holly, with apples and flowers. Throw dinner parties in her honour. Light candles. Eat well. Eat meat, and be rich, and be glad.

A FEAST FOR FREJA

So for Freja, a feast.

To welcome this goddess into your life, throw a feast: a dinner party, with your most beloved people, and your most beloved foods. Fill your life with love, and laughter, and abundance.

Take a Friday night – Frey's Day, Freja's Day – and work this magic into your life. This is the most powerful kind of spell: not really a spell at all, but a practical, no-nonsense way of really embodying the spirits and values of this great goddess.

Light gold candles; buy roses; scatter the table with flowers and stack it with heavy bowls of apples and plums.

Wear perfume; burn incense; cook succulent meats and warm spices. Drink deep, and drink often.

Wear pink, wear rich colours. Wear something that makes you feel beautiful. Wear something that makes

you feel desired, desirable and desiring. Ask someone you would like to see more of; ask the people you love to see most of. Be charming; be powerful; be a blessing. Feel your own confidence. Feel your own sensuality, and sexuality.

Do this in Freja's honour, and in your own.

Let this evening embody your home with the spirit of warmth that you wish to embrace; and keep back just one of the candles.

When you need to invoke Freja in your life, light the candle. Remember the love of your friends, and the warmth of that evening. Remember how loved you are, and send that love back out into the world.

Cast your runes with Freja's warmth in mind: a mother's advice, a lover's warning, a wife's caress. Whatever they tell you, hear them with her voice. Hear them with tenderness, sharpness, and love.

FEHU

WEALTH

*source of discord among kinsmen
and fire of the sea
and path of the serpent*

This rune is for wealth, but it literally means cattle: they were the wealth of the people, once, and still are in some parts of the world. They are money and food and fat and warmth, and they will keep us if we will keep them. Yet cattle can scatter, if you don't herd them with skill and patience. Cattle need care. Cattle need to be tended; and cattle need to be fed. This is a chance to get it right. This is a rune of new openings: of a fresh start, of a seed.

So come: you have been given a chance at beginner's mind. Let's start again. Let's leave everything behind, and fall in love for the first time. Remember what it felt like, first love? The first impression of that person, that thing, that place? The spark of new joy? The buzz of impossible, improbable luck in your veins? Feel that green energy, and hold that abundance: live in that abundance, for this moment if not longer. Hold that within you.

And yet, of course...don't hold it too tight. "A comfort to all," says

This is a rune of new openings: of a fresh start, of a seed.

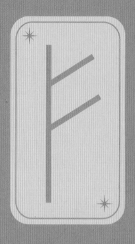

SYMBOL OF

earned income

ORIGIN OF WORD

cattle

the Anglo-Saxon version of this riddle, cheerfully, but warns– *"if bestowed freely."* The Icelandic is darker: "source of discord among kinsmen/and fire of the sea/and path of the serpent." If we don't mind our cattle, they won't mind us. If we don't give meat and milk when we have it, who will give it to us when we don't? Our luck is the luck of our people, and the luck of our place. What's good for me is good for you, too, and the other way round. What's love without people to love? What's a spark without a reason to light the fire, and what better reason to light the fire than to keep your community warm?

FEHU: REVERSED

Drawing Fehu in the reversed position could point to a financial loss if care is not taken. Sometimes it is better to admit to a mistake, take your losses and move on to another, safer project. Otherwise, you are going to find you have chosen a difficult and financially threatening path.

Fehu can also apply to emotional issues. If you are worried about a relationship, a reversed Fehu tells you that the timing may not be right. Don't let the arguments, doubts and suspicions tear you apart. Look for the deeper meaning and anticipate problems before they arise. Don't blow up small incidents out of proportion. This could be a temporary situation. A strong relationship takes a great deal of work. Give it time, patience and care, and it will become clear what you can do.

Whether it is love or wealth, a reversed Fehu is telling you that care must be taken. Be alert to situations or relationships that appear good today, but may bring problems in the future.

URUZ

WILD OX AND DRIZZLE

*lamentation of the clouds
and ruin of the hay-harvest
and abomination of the shepherd*

If Fehu brings us cattle, then Uruz
is the wild ox. Uruz is related to the
word "aurochs", a great ancestor of
our modern-day buffalo and cow.
Huge and horned, we hunted them
to extinction a long time ago, but
they live in this rune forever.

Uruz is also drizzle: small rain, rain
that soaks the hay before you
bring it in, and rain that makes
the outside just a little bit grimmer
than it needs to be. This rune is
an interruption: literally, a rainy
day. This is the rainy day you have
been saving for – so what have
you saved? The great aurochs has

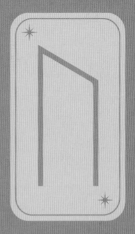

SYMBOL OF

strength and change

ORIGIN OF WORD

aurochs

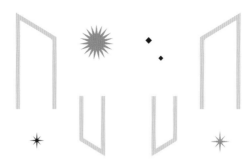

broken down your fences, and the small rain is here. How will you react to wildness?

This is something untamed; something like a bull in a china shop. Your plans are disrupted; your ambitions thwarted. Life is what happens, as they say, when you're making other plans. And this is life.

When the wild ox bursts into your world, things will get broken – but not by malice. The ox is so full of strength and heft and power that she just can't see the little things. They don't matter to her; and if you try to trap her or control her or contain her, she will be scared, and only kick harder. This is the freedom of chaos – and while it can't be avoided, it can be embraced.

Because of course, without drizzle we have no crops. Without wild oxen we have no cattle. These are vital interruptions into our lives. We have to embrace them, for without them there is no life at all.

There are projects all over the world, working to bring the aurochs back to life. Of course they were unpredictable. Of course they were too big to handle. Of course they were wild and frightening. And yet, we find, when they're gone, we miss them. And we will do anything to bring them back. We need wildness in our lives. We need beautiful chaos. Lean in, friend.

URUZ: REVERSED

You should not let an opportunity go by where you can show the world what makes you special. It takes strength to meet a challenge and overcome it. It is only natural to fear what you do not know, but have faith in yourself and you will find that courage replaces the fear.

Because Uruz is a stone of strength, it implies weakness when reversed. This takes the form of weak willpower. You may have found yourself being easily swayed lately. Those people around you who exert their own personalities may find it easy to talk you into all manner of things. It is time for you to take control of your life. You are the captain of your destiny and things never work out if you ignore your instincts. If you have

Wunjo or Gebo in your reading, it implies that your partner, whether romantic or business, is the one exerting this influence. You may perceive them as too strong for you and therefore let them have their way.

In health matters, Uruz reversed points to low vitality, which can lead to health problems or illness. Attitude has a great impact on health. If you think positively and fight against whatever ails you, you could be taking a giant step forward. Stress reduction is also a key factor. Now is the time for you to draw on your inner strength and maintain a positive outlook.

THURISAZ

GIANT AND THORN

*torture of women
and cliff-dweller
and husband of a giantess*

This letter is thorn, Thurisaz, giant. The "thurs" were great giants, once. They were husbands to their wives; and horror to all other women.

Think of Thor, the mighty, with his hammer that brings thunder. Think of his brute strength and powerful energy. Picture Thor of the Marvel movies, if you want. This works especially if you find Chris Hemsworth attractive – because this is the rune of strong male sexuality, of unbridled lust, and powerful enthusiasm that sweeps you off your feet. It's the part of the journey where the seed is planted: in other words, this is sex, fertility and impregnation.

Think also that this rune can mean, simply, thorn. Think of how a thorn embeds itself in your flesh; how it

Do the thing. Make it happen. Bend things to your will.

hooks you in; how you want to look at the pretty rose, and then the thorn catches the soft skin of your finger. When runes seem to have contradictory or multiple meanings, it's often because we're applying modern logic: a prick from a thorn

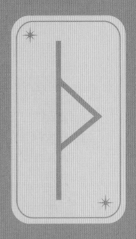

is nothing like a sexually aggressive god-giant. But think laterally. And think bawdy. Don't be too 21st century about this. It's necessary when you tell the runes to let the past into your body; to not look at their lives of blood and sex and storms with a Western, Christian-ish lens. You just *be* with them. Sit with them in what they have to tell you, and it makes a dark kind of sense. It's sometimes nice, after all, when someone says the quiet part out loud. And Thurisaz is loud. Do the thing. Make it happen. Bend things to your will.

But be kind, too, if you can. Thurisaz is not kind. You can be better.

SYMBOL OF

protection and luck

ORIGIN OF WORD

giant, thorn,
the god Thor

THURISAZ: REVERSED

Thurisaz means almost the same thing when reversed as it does upright (not that you will want to hear that). It is difficult to get someone who drew a reversed Thurisaz to listen to advice. Unfortunately, the consequences of following only your ideas, seeing only your side of things and blindly forging ahead are now worse than ever.

A reversed Thurisaz can mean that someone subordinate to you, someone you see as weaker, is causing trouble. You are seeing them as some sort of threat. This does not just apply to business, it can be found anywhere in your life. It can also be your fear that a protégé of yours is going to fail and

therefore, make you look bad. If Kenaz is in the reversed position in your reading, it is a signal that this person is about to come forward. It also indicates that you fear this person will outdo you in some way.

Your luck is running out fast, and now more than ever you need to use caution. A quick decision now is almost guaranteed to be a bad one because it is coming from weakness. It is easy to deceive yourself about your motives. This internal blindness will only worsen a situation that is already getting bad. Since you cannot rely on luck – for it is likely to be bad luck – deliberate thinking is your best weapon against further problems.

ANSUZ

A GOD

*aged Gautr
and prince of Ásgarðr
and lord of Valhalla*

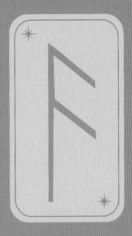

Ansuz is a god; a great god, one of the names for Odin the All-Father. This name means mouth; and it means estuary; and it means breath: the place where the river meets to the sea, and the place where the body accepts the world. This is the breath of life; and that is god. That is a great god indeed.

You see here how the double meaning makes more sense? If you start to think poetically, laterally, the patterns begin to jump out at you like a magic-eye picture. And this is the rune of patterns and poems; of logic and of lateral thinking. This is a call to think

SYMBOL OF

the spoken word,
wisdom and advice

ORIGIN OF WORD

mouth

carefully; to look before you leap, to check a map before heading out.

Ansuz asks us to think about speech. What do we say? Why do we say it? What are we hoping to get from this opening of our lips, and could we do it better? There is a divinity here. A god is stopping out of goodness to ask you: do you speak with wisdom? Do you write with care? Centre wisdom. Centre care.

RAIDO

RIDE

*joy of the horsemen
and speedy journey
and toil of the steed*

Ride! Ride on, for this is a call to action. This rune is a compass and a guide, but above all it's urging you to just go. The path is before you. The way is open. Do you need to wait? Do you need anything else, really? Or could you begin today? Those who can, do. So do it. This is a rune for adventure, and the great unknown.

Does this frighten you? It might. There's no time to plan now. You've thought about it long enough – and I bet you know, even reading this, what I'm talking about. The thing you have wanted to do. The thing you've hoped to do. Maybe you haven't even articulated it, maybe

SYMBOL OF

travel and movement

ORIGIN OF WORD

riding

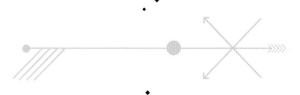

not even to yourself. But you know what it is. The secret thing you want? It's time to make it happen. It's time to go out and do it.

And sure, that might be scary. Another version of this poem notes, drily, that riding is easiest to those who don't do it and sit inside the hall.

But you're not alone here. That's the important thing. This is not a walker's rune; not a solitary traveller. This is a rider, and you have a horse. This is a rune about that trust between you and your support system. You have built the support you need with love and care; you have tamed the world so that you have allies and friends

and the helper you need on your journey. The horse will work. You know the horse will work; and indeed you may at times also be the horse. This journey will not be easy, but it will be beautiful. Toil and joy must be balanced together: this is the Ætt of balance, and you can do it.

The bond between horse and rider is like nothing else: love and service and teamwork, on both sides. The rider must care for the horse, and be trusting, and take joy. The horse must care for the rider, and be trusting, and take joy. If either is unhappy, both are unhappy. Go forward, with joy and with gratitude.

RAIDO: REVERSED

A reversed Raido warns of travel problems. You may be forced to take a trip you weren't planning. It could come at a bad time or be caused by unfortunate circumstances. A friend or relative might be sick or in trouble, and you have to drop everything to go to their side. Alternatively, it can mean that another person may visit you at a most inconvenient moment.

Unfortunately, Raido in the reversed position also says that plans and schemes you have been working on will somehow get messed up. This is therefore not the time to conduct a serious negotiation or implement an important plan, because a wrench could be thrown into the middle of it all and things could go awry. If you are aware of this possibility when you are going into the situation, then you may be able to minimize the damage. Your usually sharp mind is a little dulled right now, so try to give extra effort and thought to all of your current projects.

Lastly, be conscious of the emotional states of those around you. Tempers are going to be on edge, and it is up to you to display as much patience and humour as possible to defray some of the tension.

KENAZ

A TORCH AND A SCAR

disease fatal to children
and painful spot
and abode of mortification

Stay with me here, for the original poem is grim: this is a twin-meaning we must work hard to unpack. Kenaz is a scar, and it is a torch. It is pain, and it is joy. It is light, and it is dark.

"The torch we know by her flame", the Anglo-Saxon poem runs, "and she burns wherever bright ones sit within". This stands for illumination. It stands for the lightbulb moment: the spark in the dark. It's inspiration, and it's knowledge – knowledge that comes suddenly but seems to have been there all along. It was obvious. Of course.

A torch doesn't create the things it touches with its light: it just reveals them. The flickering beam spills over a dark room, and we see what's within. This is Kenaz: a sudden intuition to move your torch beam just here, and just there, and see what's written. You have the answers. You have them, perhaps, already within you.

For the second meaning of Kenaz, as we know, is an old wound; a sore. An ulcer. An infection. A scar. A battle mark. We must remember what infection must have meant, long ago, before antibiotics. It means death, almost certainly – unless we are lucky. Death was ever present, for the women and men who told these runes: children and warriors, the poem tells us, are

most scourged by this. Think of
the woman left behind, telling
these runes. Think of what she
knew: the depths of her pain,
the life she would lead, and still
tending her fire. Still never letting
the torch burn out.

Scars give us meaning. They give us
memory, and power. They teach us
things we would never have known
without them. Even suffering has
a purpose, and what we need is
already within us.

Perhaps, as with an infection, we
have to scrape away the old bad
flesh to see the spark of the new.
Perhaps, as in a dark room, we must
just remember to switch on the light.

SYMBOL OF
health, gifts and creativity

ORIGIN OF WORD
torch

KENAZ: REVERSED

A reversed Kenaz means the end of something. It could be a loss of love, job, friendship, marriage, position or power. This loss will have a deep meaning for you. You may blame yourself, thinking that you used bad judgement or could not see it coming. Perhaps the best way to deal with the loss is to accept it and look forward to the good things that can replace it. For instance, if the loss is your job, then perhaps there is a better job waiting for you. It can also be a good time for introspection, meditation or contemplation, as you deal with the loneliness or emptiness the loss might bring.

If your reading is generally positive, this loss may be only a short-term one. It will be more of an inconvenience or, in a relationship, a short separation rather than an actual loss.

If a delay rune, such as Isa, Hagalaz, Othala reversed or Nauthiz, appears in your reading, the loss will hinder your current progress. This will probably cause anxiety, so gather your strength.

If it is the loss of a relationship, you may have simply grown apart. Lives can separate and become distinct, easing your need for someone who once meant so much to you. You may be clinging onto this relationship. Attempting to hold onto something that is no longer working can only bring pain, so consider letting go now. It will be kinder to both of you.

GEBO

GIFT

*generosity brings credit
and honour,
which support one's dignity;
it furnishes help and
subsistence
to all broken men who are
devoid of aught else*

SYMBOL OF

partnerships, love and gifts

ORIGIN OF WORD

gift

What can you give? What should you give? If this rune has come into your life, then you are being asked to practise both gratitude and generosity: you are being asked to live as if you have enough, and then more. It's asking you to accept gifts with gratitude; it's asking you to give away what you have. Where are you withholding? Where could you be more gracious?

Gebo, or Gyfu, is the source of our word "gift". What are your gifts? What have you been given, and

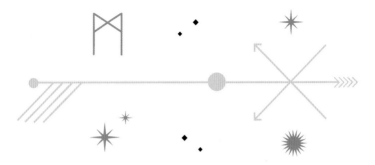

what have you been granted? And what could you give away?

You must give in order to get: you get out what you put in. This rune is a gift to you. It is a reminder that you can accept gratefully anything that is offered to you. Don't resist help, for you may need that foundation when, in turn, you are asked to give it yourself. There is a balance to this rune that is at the heart of this Ætt, and in fact at the heart of rune-telling at all.

It is sometimes associated with relationships, and has historically been associated in particular with heterosexual, male–female relationships: the balance of male energy and female energy, and the balance of giving and receiving. Remember we must think like our ancestors, without the charity of modern social mores. This is about sex, and power, and the way we must in both of those spaces remember to give just as much and more than we hope to gain.

WUNJO

JOY

*bliss he enjoys who knows
not suffering,
sorrow nor anxiety,
and has prosperity
and happiness
and a good enough house*

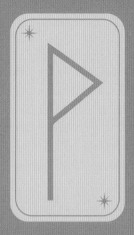

SYMBOL OF

joy and success

**ORIGIN
OF WORD**

joy

If we think of Freja's Ætt as the journey of the seed, from purchase to planting, from planting to harvest, from harvest to sale, this is the moment when we may profit. This is the moment, in fact, when we decide what to do with those profits.

The runes don't often talk of love: romantic love and familial love are outside their remit, but this comes close. This is a rune of abundance, or fruitfulness: of *enoughness*. See the last line of the poem? This is a reminder to be thankful for what you have; and not just thankful, but joyful. Rejoice in your life. Acknowledge your life, and every good thing in it. Sit with this rune, take it in your hand, and bring your focus to what you have to be grateful for. If this feels difficult to you, do it anyway. Or perhaps, do it especially. We cannot hope to be happy if we won't work for it.

It is easy to think, especially today, that happiness means something above and beyond: that in order to be happy we need a bigger house, more money, a better partner, a better job, a baby, a new car, new clothes, new anything. It is tempting to think of bliss, in particular, as something fleeting and rare. And yet...

Think again of the world these runes are speaking from: a world of death and destruction and cruel fate. In the next Ætt we will find many struggles, and many

This is a reminder to be thankful for what you have; and not just thankful, but joyful.

twists and turns, and yet here, for a moment, we can pause. The absence of suffering is, *in itself,* bliss. To be alive is bliss. To be indoors, to be safe, is bliss. This is a safe haven. Breathe it in. Recognize it; acknowledge it. Love it.

WUNJO: REVERSED

When reversed, Wunjo warns of misery and unhappiness.

The overriding message of Wunjo reversed is one of caution. If an important trip, decision or event is at hand, delay it if you can. The number six is closely related to Wunjo; so, for a more specific guideline, the delay should be six days, six weeks or six months.

Remember that everything negative can be seen as a test or an opportunity to learn. Be sincere and flexible in your dealings with others. You have a chance to turn things around because you are aware of the dangers. Drawing a reversed Wunjo means that it is time to meditate and prepare for life's battles.

The Second Ætt

INTRODUCTION TO HEIMDALL

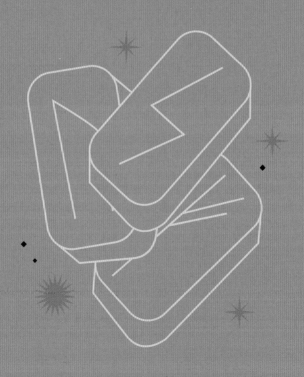

The second Ætt, that of Heimdall, are the true struggles of life: the external forces that shake us and make us. This is where we find the hail and the storm and the ice; the death and subconscious, and unconscious forces that move us. This is the Ætt of Jera, the year, and time that rolls on for *all* time; but it's also the Ætt of Perthro, the dice-throw that signifies chance and blind luck and strange fate.

When Heimdall meets humanity, it is humanity who suffers, and yet without Heimdall's runes we would never grow. It is he who keeps the mysteries that make life more than just cattle and drizzle and kisses.

Heimdall is the watchman of the gods: he stands at the doors of Valhalla and surveys the world. He is profoundly mysterious. We know even less about him than we do most of the old Norse gods, and what we know is cryptic, strange, pieced together. He carries a ram's horn, to warn of approach; and he is linked to the charging strength of the ram rampant. (Think: battering ram.) He is a warrior, and a guard. He is the "whitest of the gods"; he has "golden teeth"; needs "less sleep than a bird". He is of the wind, and the sea.

He was raised on Earth's power, and the cold sea, and the blood of a boar. These are great forces, the runes of this Ætt: they are things of deep earth and endless sea, and death, which is at the heart of life. We have death here, loss, emptiness, rebirth and the depths of our own consciousness. We have the hand of fate, and the twist of chance. We have the great World-Tree Yggdrasil, that stands for deep space; and we have Jera that stands for deep time: the way the Earth keeps on turning, and goes on and on forever. We have the basest longings of humankind, and the immortality of nature that surrounds him. These are the things that we cannot control: the things that happen to us.

WELCOMING
HEIMDALL

Heimdall, the watchman, was born to nine mothers.

Nine is a powerful number in Norse mythology. Three is sacred; and nine is three times three. There were three beings when the world was first made; three Norns, the deities that shaped the world to begin with; and Odin, king of the gods, is the third generation in his line to rule over the world.

And Odin hung from the World-Tree, Yggdrasil, for nine days and nine nights to acquire the wisdom of the universe. We have met Odin; in Heimdall's Ætt we will meet Yggdrasil. Yggdrasil is the World-Tree, the yew that touches all nine of the nine worlds; there are nine heavenly realms; and every ninth year the Norsemen would gather for nine days and nine nights, sacrificing nine men and nine beasts to the gods.

And Heimdall is the product of nine. Nine mothers, who were also nine sisters; and we think they are the nine sisters whose parents were the giants, Rán and Ægir. They live deep in the seabed, below the halls of the gods, and they are beloved of the gods. Rán translates to "Robber": she steals men down into the depths. Ægir, her husband, is simply the Ocean, and all that entails.

Their nine daughters are the nine waves of the sea: Bloody-Hair and Billow, Foam and Lift, Transparent and Cool, and three Waves that we simply have no English words to differentiate from one another. Their names are Angeyja the Harasser, Atla the Forceful, Eistla the Glowing, Eyrgjaya the Scar-giver, Gjalf the Roaring One, Greip the Grasper, Járnsaxa the Iron-knifed, and Imð and Ulfrun, the she-wolves. Here are the great threats to life,

represented as dangers so ancient we sometimes no longer see them. We have no names for the different kind of waves in English because we no longer fear them: or worse, we fear them without knowing them. We do not know our fears, and the unknown is worse still.

So let us tackle, now, the unknown fears. Let us confront the things we fear before we go into this Ætt: this Ætt of darkness and external forces that toss us to and fro. Let us, at least, know what the worst we might find there. If we control what frightens us, it cannot control us. And fear can be useful. Fear can be helpful, as pain can be a teacher: it can warn us and speak to us and let us learn about ourselves. So, let's sit with it, for a moment. Let's make space for fear.

✳

Fear can be helpful, as pain can be a teacher: it can warn us and speak to us and let us learn about ourselves.

✳

WELCOMING FEAR

Light a candle and give yourself some room to breathe.

Welcome your fear. Welcome it aloud, if you can: welcome uncertainty, and fear, and as you do it know yourself to be somewhere safe, and warm, and lit by a candle.

Say: *Fear, you are welcome here.*

Thank your fear. Thank it aloud, if you can: thank it for the warning, and the help, and the support. Thank it for everything it has given you: the gifts it has woven for you, the darkness it has helped you avoid, the sixth sense that has got you out of trouble.

Say: *Fear, I acknowledge you here. I acknowledge your gifts here; I acknowledge your power here.*

Name your fear, perhaps, if it has been nameless. Say aloud what frightens you. Say it to the candle; and say it clearly.

Say: *I am afraid...*

Look into the heart of the candle flame, and see it breathe. Breathe yourself, and as you breathe out, breathe out your fear.

Ask: *What can I do, fear, to help you?*

And listen to the answer. Is there an answer? What can you do to ease this fear – and what is the fear asking you to do? Really listen. Can you take action? Can you change anything? Is there a real threat that must be tended to, or must you simply accept it? Is your fear based in a specific worry, or a universal truth? Listen to your fear; and hear what it needs. Acknowledge the fear; accept the fear; vow that you will do all you can, and no more.

Make a solemn promise to yourself that you will do what you can control – book the doctor's appointment, open the letter from the bank, tell someone that you love them – and that the universe will do the rest. You cannot change your fate, but you can play your part. Heimdall is a watchman, and you can only watch over yourself, your community and the people you love.

Look into the candle flame, and release yourself from the pressure to do it all. Breathe out your fear, and extinguish the flame. Take the runes in your hand, and – in the smoke of your promise – begin.

HAGALAZ

HAILSTORM

*cold grain
and shower of sleet
and sickness of serpents*

There is no weather more surprisingly unpleasant than a hailstorm. Chaotic, unpredictable and stinging viciously against the skin, there is nothing to be done but take shelter. This rune signifies unavoidable disruption – and also destruction.

Think of the great hailstorms that the Vikings might have known, on the cold coasts of Scandinavia and ancient Scotland: think of the destruction huge hailstones might cause in a world where rooftops are woven thatch and the walls

The storm always breaks, in the end. The sky always clears, and we can step into it and see what the hail has left.

plastered in wattle and daub. Think of the animals killed, the children frightened, the homes destroyed. And nobody to blame for it but the universe: the universe and the gods. This is not a manmade problem, and there is no solution to it. The only thing we can do is hide. We must wait it out.

And we will wait it out. The storm always breaks, in the end. The sky always clears, and we can step into it and see what the hail has left: what shapes it has carved in the earth, what has been revealed by the sky's shattering. The "cold grain" will grow into something, if we wait: it will melt, perhaps, to soften the earth for the coming spring, and the seeds that will grow.

SYMBOL OF

damaging natural forces, disruption

ORIGIN OF WORD

hail

NAUTHIZ

NEED

*grief of the bond-maid
and state of oppression
and toilsome work*

Nauthiz, "not this", is the heavy burden of labour: of duty, necessity, and that which cannot be shirked. This is the rune of real toil. If you've pulled this rune, it might mean that this hard work is yours to shoulder: that you need to knuckle down, and get it done; that the constraints of the harness are yours, and only by wearing it

> **Nothing comes without a price, and this is a sacrifice worth making.**

will your journey succeed. In order to improve, we must work at it. Nothing comes without a price, and this is a sacrifice worth making.

But it might mean, too, to pay attention to your struggle. To honour the feeling of toil, while acknowledging our need to be free. That "bond-maid" of the poem is probably at least partly enslaved; she has no choice. She not only longs to be free, but she actively grieves that she is not. There is a longing to be free.

What oppressions are we labouring under? Can we, unlike the bond-maid, find a way out?

This rune is full of heavy choices, because the work must be done. Think of the kind of labour the bond-maid is probably employed in – subsistence farming, childcare, milking the cow and pulling the plough and keeping the home – and think of how it would feel on your hands to work like that. But think, too, of the hungry children, the cold hearth and the unploughed fields. The work must be done. Is it you who must do it? And can you do it with love, with cheer, with an understanding that there is satisfaction in meeting your need wholeheartedly?

SYMBOL OF

**need, necessity
and constraint**

ORIGIN
OF WORD

Need

NAUTHIZ: REVERSED

There are times when you make choices against the advice of others and even against your own better judgement. This could have disastrous results. Now is not the time to trample upon others or to go against your own moral code.

Think carefully about the consequences of any action. Don't act on impulse or make snap judgements. If, however, you have already started something, it is not too late. Admit to yourself that you were wrong and concentrate instead on recouping what you can. The consequence of a misguided path is despair. Your self-respect is worth more than money, prestige or sexual fulfilment.

It is even possible that a nefarious scheme you have begun will pay off – in a material sense. But don't expect to be able to sleep at night. It is imperative that you make a sincere effort to right any wrongs, regardless of the price. Otherwise, fate will deliver a severe payback.

You will become a stronger and more enlightened person if you resist this temptation. Think of this not as 'gloom and doom' but as an opportunity for unparalleled growth.

ISA

ICE

bark of rivers
and roof of the wave
and destruction of the doomed

This icicle slices through the page, single-minded and clean. This rune almost needs no translation, thinking not just of the word – so like our own– but also the clear, brutal shape of the rune itself. The ice makes a kind of spear shape on the page. And like a spear it keeps perfectly straight and true: the line is unbroken and unbending. It is a hymn of focus, control and concentration.

There is a stillness to this shape: the stillness of a frozen sea, or a frozen river. It takes those nine daughter-sister-mothers, and keeps them in check for a moment. This is a low-energy rune:

SYMBOL OF

a freeze

ORIGIN OF WORD

ice

one that warns you to conserve your energy and bide your time. This is a hard time, or hard times are coming. The rivers will freeze solid. You must be prepared, and if you are not prepared, be still. Don't waste what warmth you have left on trying to fight something as hard and cold as ice.

This is destruction, and this is doom. This is not a laughing matter. This is winter, pure and simple – and an Icelandic winter is not a good way to test yourself. This is a serious challenge, and sometimes, discretion is the better part of valour.

If you try to fight, you'll slip – and it will slip from your fingers. There's something treacherous about ice: something beautiful, too, but something that can betray you. Anyone can slip walking across it, even someone mighty or someone strong. In fact, the more forcefully you take the walk across the glacier, the more likely you are to tumble. Ice will bring you low.

So stay low. Stay small, stay humble, stay warm. Could you let this one go?

Could you sit this one out, and wait for the spring?

JERA

YEAR

*boon to men
and good summer
and thriving crops*

And Jera, the year, reminds us that spring always comes.

Spring, then summer, then the harvest: the crops thrive, and men feast, and beasts feast.

The year will always turn. We are subject to seasons, like flora and fauna. We have not, even now, invented a way to stave off the winter or bring on the summer. We are subject to time that moves whether we like it or not: an unstoppable march from the start to somewhere else, somewhere distant and beyond our gaze. We cannot escape. We cannot pause. Time is upon us, and it will

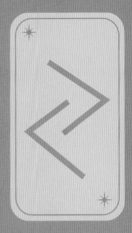

SYMBOL OF

harvest, justice, full cycle

ORIGIN OF WORD

year

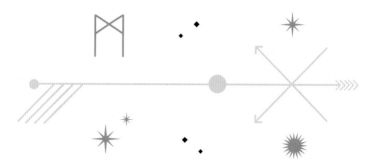

always be upon us, sweeping us somewhere that nobody knows. And so, we must learn to live in this tide. We must have patience and wait.

If we put in the time, time will bring us rewards.

This is the rune of deep time: it is the 12th rune, exactly halfway through the alphabet, making it a kind of hinge of fate. The year pivots on the harvest as the runic alphabet pivots on Jera: what we gather now will feed us until next time. We are feeding our future selves with the work we do today; and what we eat today was planted by the selves of before. Everything is connected, and nothing is lost.

Our rewards will come; and this harvest-rune is the rune of reward. It's the rune of hope and of patience, of investment and creativity and things being fulfilled. The spiral of the year brings us harvest. It will always bring us harvest, if we put in the work, if we put in the time.

If we put in the time, time will bring us rewards.

EIHWAZ

YEW

bent bow
and brittle iron
and giant of the arrow

This is the rune of Yggdrasil, the
World-Tree: it is the rune of the
yew tree. It opens the second half
of the runic alphabet, the way
yew trees traditionally mark the
entrance to a graveyard, standing
over the lychgate in a churchyard.
They have deep roots, and because
they are traditionally planted in
graveyards their roots go down
among the bodies of the dead.
They are the way to our ancestors:
to know what they knew, to see
what they saw. It is said that Odin
hung on Yggdrasil for nine days and
nine nights, no food nor water, to
understand the knowledge of the
ancients. The sacrifice was great,
but the yew tree held him safe and

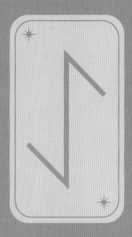

SYMBOL OF

protection, flexibility
and endurance

ORIGIN
OF WORD

yew

steady. This is the tree that keeps us rooted in the world: it goes alongside Jera, the 12th rune, to make a kind of coordinate-set of space and time.

It tells us where we are in the world: it makes a kind of compass for us. See how the rune itself looks like a two-headed arrow, pointing both up and down?

Yew trees make the best bows, and the best arrows. In Scandinavia, long ago, it is said no yew trees grew and so yew bows were prizes won from foreign lands. A yew bow will bend further than any other, and her arrows are straight and true. They land where they should land. They go where they are sent, if they are sent with purpose.

These double arrows give us direction, and if this rune appears for you it's asking you to find direction. It's asking you: where are you? Where do you want to go? Where would your ancestors want you to go? Dig deep into your own traditions, and your own sense of self and place. Be true, and be prepared to sacrifice to get there. It will be worth it. The knowledge you will gain from understanding your own journey will be worth the suffering it takes to get there.

PERTHRO

CHANCE

perthro is a source of recreation and amusement to the great, where warriors sit blithely together in the banqueting-hall

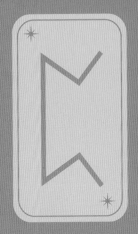

Perthro is a game of chance. It's a game of luck that represents the unknown to us. We don't know how the game was played, but we can hear the words "per throw" and see dice on a table. We know people have played dice for hundreds of years. It's a game, it's a gamble. Don't take it too seriously. Don't take anything too seriously. It's the way the warriors pass the time before battle begins. These are serious soldiers, but they play at chance like anybody else. More, perhaps, than anybody else. They know that life is for losing; and games are for winning. It's a roll of the dice, and a test of fate.

SYMBOL OF

secrets, hidden things, speculation

ORIGIN OF WORD

dice cup

But it's a hopeful rune, this one. It's amusement, it's recreation: risk it all to win it all, and risk it with a smile. You have, after all, to be in it to win it. Who knows what will happen? Tomorrow the soldiers may die on the battlefield, but tonight they feast. Tonight they dance. Tonight they play games with their friends, and even the great are invited to gamble for glory and coins. Who knows what you might win if you just put your cards down? Who knows whether this is the time you throw the double six and shimmy along to victory? You could win. You could lose, too, but who cares? You could take everything. You just have to throw those dice, and jump in.

This is a rune for risk. Take that risk.

PERTHRO: REVERSED

When Perthro is reversed, the secrets it portends are usually dark and buried. They will cause problems when exposed. They may not be your secrets, but their revelation may affect you negatively.

You may also be subject to a financial loss. It is best to avoid lending money. If you do, you may never get it back (even if it is a close friend who borrows it). To get the money returned may be an exhausting struggle and could drain you of much-needed energy. Now is not the time to visit a casino, either. Luck will be against you. Whatever natural intuition you may have will be dampened and hunches may leave you the disappointed party. For a while, things just won't be going your way.

Perthro is also associated with sex. Drawing it reversed shows incompatibility between you and your partner. This is not necessarily a permanent problem, but for a while there may be some missed cues and frustration.

Another form of secret is dark magic. However, it is best to avoid the occult right now, because it could lead to difficulties and too much negative attention.

ALGIZ

ELK-SEDGE

the elk-sedge is mostly to be found in a marsh;
it grows in the water and makes a ghastly wound,
covering with blood every warrior who touches it

Don't touch me, says Algiz. Don't come near me, and I won't come near you. Don't make me have to hurt you.

This prickly little rune wants to be left alone, and whether you heed her or not is up to you. Everything has consequences, but you have free will: you can do as you please. This rune wants to think about boundaries: your own, and other people's, and the boundaries set by nature herself. The elk-sedge grows deep in the marsh, where no man has a right to be. She has taken herself away from people, and if people come anyway, then – so? So what if they get hurt?

This rune wants real compassion – for everyone in the story. Boundaries matter, but lashing out is almost never the best option. Being left hurt is terrible, but so is being touched and plucked and picked when you've tried your best to get away.

This rune says: are you overstepping someone's boundaries? Is someone overstepping yours?

Could you draw some boundaries for yourself? Could you make sure there are consequences to your boundaries being overridden? You have a right to protect yourself. You have a right to ask for what you need, remember. You deserve space, and time – but you don't have to lash out. Can you think of a way to draw boundaries that doesn't leave people bleeding? Is there a kinder way to ask? Is there a better way to make it happen?

Or perhaps you're the person left bleeding. Should you have stepped back? Can you give this rune the space she needs? Can you respect people's choices, and ask them to respect yours?

SYMBOL OF

protection, friendship and defence

ORIGIN OF WORD

protection/defence, elk, sedge grass

ALGIZ: REVERSED

Algiz reversed is a warning that you need to look at what others are gaining from your hard work. Opportunistic acquaintances may have made you the scapegoat for their failures. Algiz reversed also warns that you might be deliberately misled or deceived. You may be at a weak and vulnerable time in your life. It is this weakness that is allowing others to take advantage of you.

Your judgement may be clouded. Look critically at what others want from you. Now would be a good time to review the actions of your partner. If you discover dishonesty, then determine what your partner wants. This knowledge can work to your advantage. Whether or not you choose a confrontation, at least you will not be blindly trusting.

Algiz reversed also functions as a mirror. You may find that you are the cause of your own problems. Are you trying to get something for nothing? If it looks too good to be true, it probably is.

Letting others find your answers for you rarely works, because you can end up being cheated. Awareness of yourself, your potential and the people in your life is one way to gain control. You can lose this control if you are taken in by glib strangers. Pay close attention to what is really happening. Only when you are aware of problems can you create solutions.

SOWILO

SUN

*shield of the clouds
and shining ray
and destroyer of ice*

In the Anglo-Saxon version of this poem, we hear that Sowilo is the "hope of sailors"; in the Icelandic, we hear this rune is the "destroyer of ice". The nine dangerous waves have become sparkling and beautiful in the light of the Sun; the ice and the hail have melted. This is the Sun that guides sailors to land, after their long nights and dark storms: this is the Sun that clears infection and brings colour to our cheeks and fat fruitfulness to the harvest. The shining ray lights us up, even in winter.

We sit with it, and feel the hardships melt away like ice itself.

Think of those long, dark Icelandic winters, and how good it must have felt to finally see the Sun. This is Heimdall's hope for us, after everything we've been through: after all the struggles and toil and work. This is victory. This is mastery. This is a blaze of sunlight,

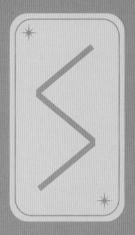

a fire flickering in a hearth, the return of warmth to frozen hands and feet.

We sit with it, and feel the hardships melt away like ice itself. This is the comfort zone, and sometimes we have to allow ourselves time to be there. Relax a little bit. There is safety here: safety and comfort and joy.

SYMBOL OF

victory, energy and health

ORIGIN OF WORD

sun

INTRODUCTION TO TYR

The last Ætt, that of Tyr, are the internal forces that keep us afloat: that keep us together in the face of those trials and keep us from being more than just simple beasts. This is the place where visible and invisible come together; the place where community and strength of character and spirit come shining through to the forefront. Here is the god Tyr, who sacrificed his hand to the world-eating wolf; and with him we find willpower and triumph; traditions and home-building and the upcoming dawn. He is justice. He is honour.

Tyr is Tiw, or Teiwaz. He is the French *dieu*, and our own "deity". His day is Tuesday: *Dienstag*, in German, and *Dinsdag* in Danish. These translate, roughly, to "Thing Day". The word "thing" has such a vague and wide meaning in today's English, but it used to mean something much more. Once, "Thing" meant a gathering, and a gathering of free people coming

together to meet and discuss and make laws and mete justice. This is the first part of the meaning of Tyr: his day is Thing Day, the day of the folkmoot, or assembly. His day is the day of community; of the traditions of man, of our home, of our people, and the structures we build to keep ourselves together.

And yet the story of Tyr is also more than that. What we can learn from Tyr, who is both master of the Ætt and a rune in his own right, are all the forces that let us make those structures and communities in the first place. It is the Ætt of self-sacrifice, of our subconscious, of justice and love and the new day. Of beginning again. Tyr sacrificed his hand so that the world might not end, and this is the story we have to tell to see the full force of this Ætt.

Now, to understand Tyr, we have to understand his world: the world of the gods, giants and their complex web of sex and death and murder and glory. It is not our world. When we try to impose our own ideas on it, it becomes both maddening and a little bit silly. It is said that to really understand the literary power of the great Western classics, you must become a Christian while you read them: you have to really believe in and understand the stakes of that world. The same is true here. You have to go with it.

This story happened in the past, but it also happens in the future. It is the story of the end of the world, our world, and the death of the gods. And it is, too, the story of their rebirth, and ours.

The trickster-god Loki has three children by the giantess Anguish-bringer: a great serpent named Jormungard, a death-goddess named Hel and a fierce wolf named Fenrir. And the other gods believe that they are trouble. And, of course, they are right.

The gods know that these three, together with their father, will bring about the end of the world. Loki will kill the god Baldur – beloved by all, shining and joyful – by a trick; Hel refuses to let him out of the underworld. And, quite literally, all hell breaks loose. The world is at war. Brothers fight sisters; mothers fight children. Gods are cut down where they stand, and even mighty Odin is eaten by the serpent Jormungard. Everything is in despair; the sky is rent in two; and Fenrir, the wolf, promises to devour all things that remain. This is Ragnarok: the endtimes. There will be nothing left, then, except a need to begin again. From this broken world, a man and a woman will emerge from the last wood standing. The daughters and sons of the gods will emerge. The Sun will shine again. And the world will start anew.

To give us a little more time, however, the gods have kept these three children at bay. They send

Hel down to her own namesake domain, to keep guard there. They cast the serpent into the sea. And yet nobody knows what to do with Fenrir. The great wolf cannot be left unsupervised, even as a pup – and so Tyr, fearless, loyal Tyr, takes the wolf cub for his own. He feeds him. He raises him. He gives him meat from his own hand.

And as the wolf grows, so too does the threat. The gods decide that Fenrir must be chained; and to trick him into submission they tell him the chains are a trial, to prove his great strength. They swear an oath to it. Fenrir, suspicious, says that he will succumb to the chains only if Tyr will put his hand in his mouth. If he cannot break free from the chains, he will swallow Tyr's sword hand.

And Tyr does it. The wolf bites his hand; and he is broken forever; but the world is saved. He gave so that we might live, and this is his Ætt: reasons to live, and what to live for.

✳

This is the place where visible and invisible come together; the place where community and strength of character and spirit come full shining to the forefront.

✳

WELCOMING
TYR

Let us take this time, now, to understand what we have to live for.

It can be easy, in the chaos of life, to lose sight of what it is that matters: when we work all day, what is it that we're working for? What is it that drives us to do what we do?

Tyr takes on the burden, not just of placing his hand in the wolf's mouth, but of caring for the wolf at all. He sees what has to be done for his community, and does it: and this is why his day, Tiw's day, is also *Dienstag*. He rules "Thing Day", when people came together, and they did it with joy and for justice. Things, in the old sense, were how we evolved away from wars; how we stopped warring clans, and blood feuds, and vengeance. We came together under the aegis of Tyr to speak our minds: to hear and be heard. It is said that at Things, any free man might put forward their case. Anyone had the right to speak, and everyone had a duty to listen. And these Things were a joy. There was feasting, and marriages, and money. There was sex, and there was power, and there was, too, a kind of balance. Anyone might come. Anyone might speak. Anything might be decided, and all could be seen for what they really were.

If a thing is an object, it's an object that has been noticed. "That thing," we say, about something we have seen even if not yet known or named. "This thing here," we say, indicating that we want someone else to see. "The thing is," we say, to indicate the point of a matter. It's an all-purpose word for an all-purpose god: because community, and noticing the heart of our community, never goes out of style.

Tyr is a god of community: of togetherness, and in his honour we must contemplate our role in the world: our place in our community. We thrive when we belong.

FINDING WHERE YOU BELONG

You can think of this exercise as a kind of secular prayer - or feel free to dedicate it to any god you believe in, including Tyr. You might want to write down any words and thoughts that occur to you as you contemplate these questions.

Ask yourself:

Where do I belong?
What matters to me?
Who matters to me?

These are big questions, but they are the questions that Tyr's story asks of us. It asks us to keep our people and our values at the forefront in our mind, and live up to them. He also asks us to extend that community out, not just our friends, and not just our family, but to the wider world. He loses his hand not just for the gods, but for all mankind; and the Things that happen on his day are to bring together all kinds of diverse clans and communities. We are happiest, as people, when we come together.

Ask yourself:

Where could my life be more diverse?
Where could I bring together my community?
How could I strengthen your bond to my community?

Does this feel daunting? It might do. Here's the thing (!): you have to reach out to your community so that your community can reach out to you. You might volunteer at a library; join a running club as a marshal; write to your elected representative to push for change. You might talk to a neighbour; or offer to help weed the flowerbeds in a neighbourhood park. You might simply look at a local noticeboard and see if anything jumps out at you. There will be somewhere, somehow, for you to belong. If you take the time to plant a seed, and water it, something beautiful might just grow.

And Tyr asks us to ask ourselves:

What can I do to help?

TEIWAZ

TYR

*god with one hand
and leavings of the wolf
and prince of temples*

We have just heard the story of Tyr, who is Teiwaz. This is the rune of the Ætt: the rune that carries most the sense of justice, righteousness and sacrifice. Look at the straight spear point of the rune itself: the rune doesn't waver, and nor can we.

Tyr knows, even as he puts his hand in Fenrir's mouth, what will happen.

He *knows* that the chain is unbreakable, but he knows that his wolf cannot roam free any longer. He *knows* that the gods have lied to the wolf, but he knows that someone always has to pay for a bargain made under duress. He *knows* that for justice to be served, he must lose something precious.

To save the world, he must give up his ability to fight. To save the honour of the gods, he must make their oath a fair trade: his strength for Fenrir's strength, his fight for the world's fight. This is a bargain.

He was loving; he was brave; he was loyal.

This is justice. And he does it.

And what's more, he does it for the wolf he himself fed. He fed

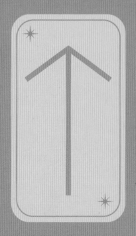

the wolf; he nourished it. He gave it the chance to be loved, and to be safe. And when it became a danger to everything and everyone, he was there at the end, too. He was there when the wolf was a pup, and he was there when the wolf was banished. He took responsibility, every time. He did not turn his back.

He was fair; he was just. He fed the cub; he bound the wolf; he risked his life and gave his right arm to do it. He was loving; he was brave; he was loyal. He knew his community, and he knew what they needed. How can you carry this spirit into your life? What must you give to see justice done? What sacrifice could you make to see freedom happen?

SYMBOL OF
victory, the fighting spirit, law and order

ORIGIN OF WORD
the god Tyr (Tiw), spear

TEIWAZ: REVERSED

Do you feel lethargic? Have you lost faith in yourself? To be a winner, you must believe that you are brimming with undiscovered potential. Don't let the apathy and drudgery of a reversed Teiwaz define you. Fight your negative feelings, think positive, and you will be surprised how quickly things change.

You might feel as though your creative juices are not flowing, that you are unfocused and prone to self-pity. This is temporary. Look for the positives in your life and, most importantly, work to regain focus.

In romance, a reversed Teiwaz warns of obstacles in your relationship. You say one thing, and your partner another. Listen closely, however, because sometimes you are both making the same statement but using different words. If the relationship is worth saving, it may be up to you to call a truce. But be careful, because a complete confession of your inner heart may be too overwhelming. Reveal your feelings to your partner gradually, so as not to strain the relationship. Blurting out the entire truth will leave your partner either powerless or with fresh ammunition. Work together and love can be reborn.

BERKANA

BIRCH GODDESS

*leafy twig
and little tree
and fresh young shrub*

Here is a green, quiet place, after all the blood and fighting. Here is somewhere safe, and somewhere special. A beautiful place. A place that knows itself, and knows you, too. There is something almost motherly about this place: the young trees growing up and around each other, little shoots, new leaves, things just coming into bud. And there is space for you here, too. The sound of wind in the canopy, and the burble of a stream somewhere below. There is no need to talk. Just rest, here, in the green of the birch grove.

Berkana is a birch tree, and a goddess: she brings spring, and rebirth, and secrets.

SYMBOL OF

fertility and family

ORIGIN OF WORD

birch twig

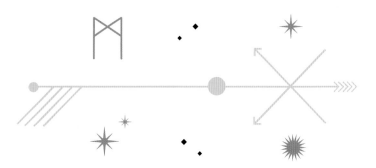

Her secrets are her own, the way a pregnant woman first might keep her own counsel. This is personal, and this is special. There is a gentle kind of privacy to this rune that encourages you to know your own mind, but speak it only where necessary. There is no need to fight. There is no need for war. The birch grove grows up quickly, and covers the earth with tiny suckers, and puts down roots fast. Where there was war, there is now a little forest. Peace can come, if we wish for it: we must wish for it, and work for it, and make space for it. Let the little shoots grow where they will. Progress should leave room for the old ways, and the new moments to emerge. When we try too hard, we drown out things that we could have had all along. Why not stop fighting?

Why not lay down your weapons, and give in to the serenity of this little leafy place?

Carry the spirit of Berkana with you, if you can. Keep that calm in your mind: that private, gentle reserve. Birch sap can be drunk – like cool water, but sweet – if you tap the tree right. Rich in minerals, it can save you, if you're lost and you're thirsty. Drink deep from this birch grove, and wonder: what lies within you? What sap can you save, and keep back for yourself? What peace can you bring with your silence, your counsel, your calm?

BERKANA: REVERSED

A reversed Berkana shows that you might be at odds with your family. This is not a dire warning so much as a caution. Remember, these people are your support system. You are not compelled to agree with what they say, but don't alienate them. Talk to them and work towards understanding. If you can accomplish this, the rift will be short-lived.

Berkana reversed can also be a warning that trouble is on the way. There is the potential of something going wrong in the near future. There are even indications that someone in your family might experience an illness or succumb to a 'disease of the spirit'. For the latter condition, kindness, understanding and unwavering support are yours to give.

If you have also drawn Gebo, the person you will most likely be concerned about will be your spouse or partner. With Ansuz it will be a child, and with Othala an older relative, such as one of your parents.

Pertaining to business, a reversed Berkana counsels caution. Your business will be safe as long as you practise good judgement, preparedness and timing. Don't discard your idea; rather, make sure you are ready for it. Just as you would not go to the opera wearing shorts (you would take the time to find out the correct attire), so you need to pay attention to your career. Do your homework and if things get put off for a short while, it is all right. Things could just work out better this way.

EHWAZ

HORSE

a horse is a joy to princes in the presence of warriors.
a steed in the pride of its hooves,
when rich men on horseback bandy words about it;
and it is ever a source of comfort to the restless

Remember Raido? Remember the rider, and the ride? Here is the other side of that rune: Ehwaz, the horse, and the thrill of it all. This is swiftness; this is joy. This is pure pleasure in your most animal self: moving and running and galloping on. Give no thought to the destination; give no thought to anything but the pull of the future, and hooves on the ground. Have pride in how far you can go, and how far you will go. Don't hesitate. Don't "bandy words" about it. This isn't the rider, this isn't the "rich man", but the horse itself.

This, too, is a rune for adventure – and just like the rune for the rider,

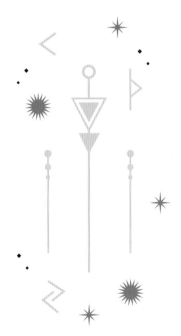

it's a rune about love. It's a rune about trust, and love, and your companion coming with you. It's about trusting the person you've decided to trust and falling in hard: about going with them wherever they've decided to go. It's about finding joy in that bond; and pride in that bond.

Restlessness can be a curse, and it need not be: you can cure it. You can cure it by moving, by getting up and going. Don't talk any more. Don't think any more.

Be restless with pride. Go forth.

SYMBOL OF
movement and loyalty

ORIGIN OF WORD
horse

EHWAZ: REVERSED

Ehwaz reversed is not necessarily negative. Unlike most runes, it does not significantly change its meaning when reversed, with one or two exceptions.

A reversed Ehwaz indicates that you may be presented with an opportunity that is not necessarily the best thing for you at this time. Examine it closely. Is it a step forward, or does it really mean that you are standing still, or even taking a step backwards? If so, you should trust that something better will come along soon.

If you have a generally negative reading, Ehwaz is a warning to hold fast. This may not be the time for you to make any major changes in your life. They may complicate things and potentially damage the status quo. Be honest, because

if you are true to yourself, you are seldom wrong. Ehwaz does not talk about a timetable when things will get better. It is best to wait and see what happens. Your natural insight will lead you to the problem that, once solved, will change everything.

When paired with some runes, a reversed Ehwaz can indicate a distant journey. With Laguz, you will most likely travel by air. If you drew Raido, the journey is for recreation. With Fehu, it's an essential business trip. With Uruz, a change may come that will take you completely by surprise. However, Uruz's portent for change may be a detrimental one, if you have a negative reading.

MANNAZ

MAN

*delight of man
and augmentation of the earth
and adorner of ships*

Mannaz is man, and man is the
"delight of man". What a simple
and lovely phrase: man is the
delight of man! We need our
friends, we need our people, we
need our community. We are all
we have, on our ships and on the
Earth: on land and at sea, we have
only each other.

We have only each other, and
the world we build together. We
make traditions to keep ourselves
anchored in time and space; to
make this crazy universe feel more
like a home. Let it feel like a home.

Life is short, and life is hard. Death
is inevitable; and the cold march of
the years goes on, and the Earth

SYMBOL OF

humankind and
interdependence

ORIGIN
OF WORD

humankind

keeps on turning. And yet, in the face of all this eternity, we have each other. We have each other, and the things we make.

We have only each other, and the world we build together.

Cherish your friends; cherish your family; cherish your community. Cling to your people like you're in a ship in a storm; and hold out a hand to the people you haven't met yet. Find a way to belong where you are. Put down roots. Put out buds. Reach out to one another.

We are little points of light in a vast, uncaring universe, and yet we are all still here, and together we can come together, and we will blaze.

MANNAZ: REVERSED

Mannaz reversed indicates that you are standing alone, without help from anyone. Whether it is a group or a single person, you may have an enemy or a detractor. Don't be paranoid, but be aware of what is going on around you. Blind trust without any awareness is not serving you at this time.

Sometimes a reversed Mannaz can mean you are your own worst enemy. Self-doubt or a gloomy outlook on life can make things seem worse than they really are. Conceit or stubbornness may be to blame, or it could just be a generally negative attitude. Try to see things from another person's perspective. Do your best to acknowledge all the positive things in your life. With practice, you can begin to shake off that pervasive gloom.

Your life may have a strange, foreign feel to it. You may have recently moved house or returned from a place where customs are different. Perhaps there is someone whose thoughts and actions seem strange or foreign to you. Whatever the case, the differences between you will cause anxiety. You may be timid, fearing you will offend this person with your behaviour or make a cultural error. Yet there is the fascination of being with someone so different. The outcome of this relationship will depend on your ability to readjust and synthesize yourself back into society.

LAGUZ

LAKE

*eddying stream
and broad geysir
and land of the fish*

This is the rune of the subconscious, and the unconscious mind. The water here is the water of life, and it flows in all of us. We are made up, as people, mostly of water, and this rune invites you to sink into yourself. Water is always associated with dreams and imagination: the soft clouds of what might be, what we wish, what we hope, what we fear. Acknowledge those dreams; accept those fears. Find out what you know. Find out what you have within you.

And remember, too, that the early rune-tellers were Vikings. They were ship people, sailors and adventurers, and they lived on islands swept up in sea storms and buffeted by rain and hail, threaded with streams and geysers and tumbling falls. Water was their

Acknowledge those dreams; accept those fears. Find out what you know. Find out what you have within you.

world, and they saw in it everything from salvation to despair. Too much water is a deadly poison; too little will leave you at best

confused and at worst a corpse. It can drown you, or sweep you along in its thrall. It can be icy cold, or scalding steam. It can be clouds, salt oceans, a storm at sea or the sap of a birch grove. It is the land of the fish: a whole home, a world that is somehow both our own and perfectly alien at the same time. This rune reminds us that we are part of everything; and everything is part of us. We are our own salvation, and our own despair.

Look with yourself: what's there? What dreams? What depths?

SYMBOL OF

intuition and
your inner voice

ORIGIN
OF WORD

water

LAGUZ: REVERSED

When Laguz is reversed, you have an inner voice that is giving you bad advice. Through either ego or conceit, you are now in way over your head. It is time to be honest with yourself and re-evaluate the situation.

You might be trying to shift responsibility to another's shoulders. Unless you face things head on and take all the necessary steps, you will be caught. You could lose more than money, love or prestige: you are in danger of losing your self-respect. Step back from the problem, ignore your inner voice and look at this as if you were an outsider. What would a stranger think?

Be truthful with yourself, know your limitations yet strive to extend them. Pay attention to what is really going on around you, look closely at the motivations of others, and avoid the easy solution. You have what it takes.

If you have an extremely positive runecast, most of the sting is taken out of Laguz reversed. Major areas of your life will not be affected. Only minor, possibly frustrating, inconveniences will result, and not dire consequences. Be patient with yourself and others and you will succeed.

INGUZ

THE SEED AND THE LORD

*Inguz was first seen by men
among the East-Danes,
till, followed by his chariot,
he departed eastwards
over the wave
and so they named the hero*

Inguz, or Yngvi, is the twin brother of Freja, and is as richly steeped in love and pleasure as she is. They call him Freyr, which means "lord", and he is a lord: a hero and a king, master of fertility and pleasure and power.

He rides a boar; he owns a ship into whose sails the wind always blows. He is peace and pleasure; he is the rain and the Sun when they come in contentment and moderation. He is shining, and golden, and – famously – prodigiously endowed. He is an old-school fertility god, and this rune asks about that

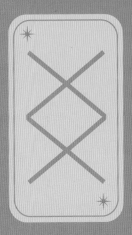

SYMBOL OF

completion and
new beginnings

ORIGIN OF WORD

the god Ing

masculine sexuality: ask for what you want, and know you will be given it, and know, too, that you will give pleasure when you do. Know your own power, and your own worth, and your own charm.

Don't be foolish with it: don't give away what you can't get back. Inguz gave his sword to win a giantess and came to regret it.

But don't worry too much. This is a rune not of struggle, but of sex and joy and love and abundance. This is a rune of things planted and things coming to fruition. If Berkana carries within herself that secret, pregnant joy, Inguz is her male counterpart. He is the father, the hero, the rich, comfortable, male sexuality that balances out her beautiful feminine peace.

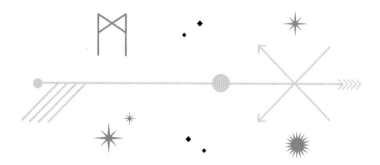

OTHALA

HOME

an estate is very dear to every man,
if he can enjoy there in his house
whatever is right and proper
in constancy and prosperity

And following Inguz, the father, comes this rune: Othala. Othala here means "home"; but the word Othala is related to "Atilla", which means "little father". Take your cues from this: Othala is a rune of small places and warm places and endearments. It is a rune of great wealth, and something like love. This is the rune of our inheritance – what we take from our parents, and give to our children.

This is the rune of our cultural identity, whatever and wherever that may be.

Like a few other runes, it's often been co-opted by people who

SYMBOL OF

**material possessions,
character and inheritance**

ORIGIN OF WORD

possession

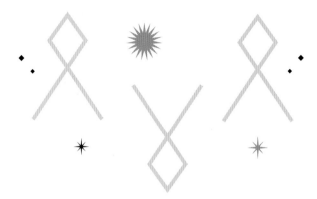

think there is only one valid kind of cultural inheritance. This is ridiculous, dangerous and incorrect. This rune speaks to us, whoever we are, and whatever we inherit, and whatever we wish to pass on. This is a rune of love, of home and of hope.

We build our homes to make safe spaces for the people we love, and for ourselves. We build them with what we believe to be right; what we believe to be proper. We make them out of our morals, and our work, and the things we bring from our past. Our burdens here can be set down; our wild oxen tamed; our running horse given hay and water, and a stable to rest. Here we can shelter from the storm, and bring in our harvest. Here we can plant the birch grove. Here we can set down our swords, and let our scars heal. Here we can sleep.

Let yourself rest, love. Let yourself have a little time. Come inside, come by the fire, and be warm. Be loved. Be safe, and sleep.

OTHALA: REVERSED

Othala reversed is usually a sign of frustration and delay. You may be trying to move too fast. If you persist on going at high speeds, you may destroy any chance of reaching your goals. If you have an otherwise positive reading, you will probably achieve them. It will simply take you a little longer than you estimated.

The timetable you have set may be out of step with reality. Don't be so hurried that you can't see opportunities. Rushing from project to project, or relationship to relationship, can blind you. Given the proper amount of time, things will fall into place. If something is immediate, remember to pay close attention to details. Brushing aside the essential, but time-consuming, details is the surest way to sabotage anything that has great potential.

You might be standing alone. Your haste, actions and goals may have alienated you from your friends, family or business associates. Unfortunately, help will not be forthcoming from the usual places in which you have sought it in the past. Money won't help you out of the fix you may be in, either. Sincerity will get you a lot farther than a cheque. Honesty will win the day.

Now is the time to slow down and implement a more conservative approach. This may be all you need to fix things. If not, it is an excellent place from which to start. Let your inner truths show, and it will be difficult for anyone to resist.

DAGAZ

DAWN

day, the glorious light of the Creator, is sent by the gods;
it is beloved of men, a source of hope and happiness to rich and poor,
and of service to all

And when we have slept, the dawn will always come. Over the horizon, no matter how dark the night, illumination rises: enlightenment comes, and every puzzle can be solved. In time, light returns – and not so much time, either. There are 24 hours in a day, and 24 runes in an alphabet, and that's not so long to wait for a fresh start.

Jera, the year, promises an endless tide of time – but sometimes you need a new slate just a little quicker than that. The things you do today may be gone tomorrow; the mistakes you made yesterday

may be washed clean, or seen anew in a better light, this morning.

Know that at the end of the day, if nothing else, you will sleep; and a new day will come no matter what.

This is not slow change; this is not the steady turn of the wheel of the year. This is the morning, coming at you in your own bed. What can you do? What will you do? Tend your projects. Love your people. Know that at the end of the day, if nothing else, you will sleep; and a new day will come no matter what.

The dawn comes every day, and every day is useful. Every day can be *made* to be useful.

This rune, the last rune, gives you the world and asks you what you will make of it. What will you do with your life? That's too big a question for most of us.

What will you do with your day?

What *could* you do with your day?

SYMBOL OF

prosperity, growth and security

ORIGIN OF WORD

day

USING RUNES FOR POSITIVE CHANGE

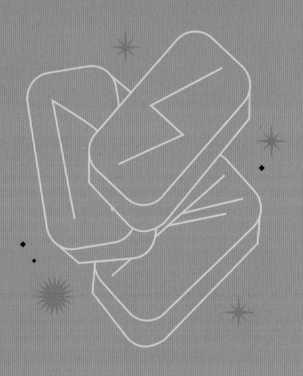

UNDERSTANDING YOURSELF

To tap into the divine mysteries embodied by the runes, it is important to first have a sense of understanding about yourself. To achieve this, you can use the runes themselves as your guide.

Because there is no way to know exactly how the ancient runemasters laid out their stones, modern runecasters have borrowed from other divinatory sources, such as the Tarot and the I-Ching. These other spreads work well with the runes, but this modern 'borrowing' means that layouts are open to interpretation, new forms and your own insightful imagination. Feel free to create your own layouts that specifically respond to your concerns, questions and lifestyle. Choose a layout that is as simple or as complex as you prefer. You can ask a yes or no question and draw a rune. If it is upright, the answer is yes. If it is reversed, it is no.

If it is a rune without a reverse, you can either assume you must ask the question later or draw another stone.

To begin your voyage of self-discovery, ask the runes if the time is right. When you have concentrated on this question, shake your rune pouch to mix up the stones and then reach into the bag, sifting through them until one piece 'feels' like the answer. Pull it out and see if it is upright or reversed. If your runes have no clear north–south orientation, and your rune is sideways, move it one-quarter clockwise. If it is upright, it is time to begin. Replace the stone.

One-stone reading:
'WHO AM I?'

Focus on a new question. Ask the runes who you are at this moment in your life. This will be your 'base'. It may tell you the positive things you bring to the world, or it could highlight some of the challenges in your life. You will be the best person to interpret how its meaning applies to your question. Pull a new stone from the bag.

SAMPLE READING:
Upright Ehwaz

Ehwaz is the rune that stands for 'horse' and signifies travel, movement and loyalty. Let's pretend for a moment that as you begin on your spiritual path of self-discovery, you drew this stone.

You might feel that some details of the Ehwaz interpretation details hit home, while others don't appear to apply as neatly. This is normal. Not every truth is self-evident, so the hidden aspects may become clearer with time. Sometimes you pull a stone for one statement or aspect that resonates deeply within you. If you need to hear something, the runes will tell you, even if you were not expecting that answer. Keep an open mind.

Nearly any question can be answered with a single stone. The answer may not be complex, but the rune will give you insights.

Upright Ehwaz

Three-stone reading:
'WHERE AM I?'

It is important to get a sense of where you are in time and this means gaining insight into how you to got to where you are today, your present circumstances and a glimpse into a possible future. For this, you can use the layout of the Norns, showing the past, present and future.

For learning's sake, I'll draw three runes and we'll pretend that they apply to you. In this way you will see what different thought processes you need to go through as you use the runes.

1 past:
reversed
Raido

2 present:
upright
Kenaz

3 future:
Jera

Jera is a cycle rune, and a symbol of the harvest. It shows a reaping of rewards from hard work.

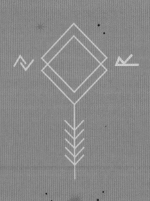

SAMPLE READING:
Reversed Raido, upright Kenaz, Jera

Here the past shows a reversed Raido, the present shows an upright Kenaz and the future shows Jera, a stone with no reverse.

The reversed Raido speaks of difficulties in the past, possibly involving travel or perhaps indicating a plan that went awry. If these were the stones you drew, you should study the description of Raido in this book, both upright and reversed, to familiarize yourself with the symbol and its meanings. Then you should contemplate how the message of the reversed Raido applies to you. When you feel the resonance of the rune, and its message, it is time to move on to the stone sitting in the 'present' position.

An upright Kenaz is a wonderfully positive rune. Again, if this reading were about you, you would study the meaning and apply it to your life. Drawing Kenaz, a rune of health, creativity and relationships, would probably mean these things are a focus in the present. Think about what is going on in your life, and try to discern those places in which the rune description and your life events intersect.

Think about the effect a reversed Raido in the past might have on an upright Kenaz in the present. Can you see a correlation? Can you see the flow of one rune to another, and how they can influence each other? These are the kinds of questions you should ask yourself when you do your own reading.

Finally, it is time to examine the rune that landed in the future, or result, position. This is Jera, a rune with no reverse. Jera is a cycle rune, and a symbol of the harvest. It shows a reaping of rewards from hard work.

Putting all three stones together, there is a pattern of missed opportunities leading to a focus on personal creativity, which results in the reaping of rewards. This is a kind of roadmap that your life may have followed, had these been the runes you drew.

Like the one-stone read, you can ask any question and use the three-stone layout. It gives a quick, yet more detailed answer than a single rune, and is an excellent way to get an overview of where you or another questioner stands in time.

Four-stone reading:
'WHAT ARE MY STRENGTHS AND CHALLENGES?'

Now that you know who and where you are, it is time to take a more detailed approach to flesh out the simple answers. A four-stone reading would work well here. Designed to help you discover your current condition, this layout points out your strengths and weaknesses, as well as obstacles and possible sources of support. When you pull the runes, start at the bottom and place each subsequent rune clockwise around the layout until you have all four.

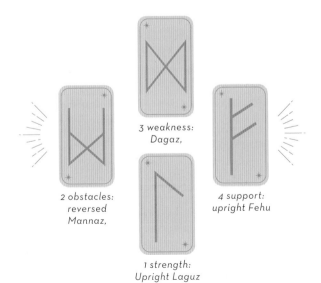

3 weakness: Dagaz,

2 obstacles: reversed Mannaz,

4 support: upright Fehu

1 strength: Upright Laguz

SAMPLE READING:
Upright Laguz, reversed Mannaz, Dagaz, upright Fehu

Jenny is at a crossroads in her life and wants to know what strengths and challenges she has. Using the four-stone reading, she received an upright Laguz in the strength position, a reversed Mannaz in obstacles, Dagaz in weakness and an upright Fehu in the support position.

Starting with Laguz in the strength position, it is easy to see that Jenny's strengths are creativity, imagination and intuition – a wonderful set of skills to bring to the world – and it is also easy to see why these would be considered strengths.

Travelling clockwise from Laguz, we find a reversed Mannaz in the obstacles position. This rune speaks of self-doubt, conceit, a gloomy outlook or the presence of an enemy. These are the things standing in Jenny's way.

From obstacles, we go to weaknesses and see Dagaz. Because Dagaz is such a strong, positive rune, Jenny didn't understand how it could show weakness. The idea is to read the information on Dagaz knowing that it is talking about a weakness. The positives it espouses are most likely things that are within her grasp, if she can overcome her vulnerabilities. For example, it speaks of earning rewards from hard work. Is Jenny working hard enough or is she dreaming of rewards while being unwilling to do the work? Perhaps she is dwelling on her problems and attracting more to her. This is another weakness that must be overcome.

Now that she has seen strengths and weaknesses, along with obstacles, it's time to explore what kind of support she can expect. The final rune is an upright Fehu, which shows that there is support out there. Interestingly, this rune also speaks of rewards after hard work. Because this concept came up twice, Jenny needs to look at this as a possible issue. Fehu also gives information on relationships – another good source of support.

When Jenny finished exploring each individual rune's meaning, she then looked at the reading as a whole and gained valuable insight into her strengths and challenges. She is now aware of what she needs to do to achieve her goals. Like Jenny, you too can gain a powerful perspective with this layout.

USING THE LAYOUTS

A journey of self-understanding is an excellent way to begin your relationship with the runes. The more you understand, the better the runes will serve you. One way to keep in touch with this self-understanding is to start every day with a quick one-rune reading, asking 'Who am I today?'. This will give you a barometer for the day, helping you to understand some of the actions and reactions you will experience as the day progresses.

At the end of the day, a three-stone 'Where am I?' reading could help you process the day's activities. How did your experiences that day affect you? Were there any hidden lessons that you needed to learn? The runes may be able to shine a light on thoughts and events that you had not fully integrated. If you are faced with a difficult decision, a check of your strengths and challenges might give you the insight you need to make up your mind. If you pull delay runes, it can tell you that the decision is better left to another time, when you are stronger and more capable of making a decision that is beneficial to everyone involved.

Once you have finished the exploration of your inner self, it will be time to move on to new explorations. In the next section, you will see how to guide your present life using a new set of layouts, both large and small. You will see many of the same runes that were shown in this section, but their interpretations will depend on the questions asked and also on their positions in the layouts. I hope this will help you when you begin to ask your own questions and draw your own runes.

✳

The more you understand about yourself, the more the runes will serve you.

✳

GUIDING YOUR PRESENT LIFE

When many people seek the advice of an oracle, they are primarily concerned about something specific that is occurring in their life at that moment. These include questions about health, relationships, finances, careers, spirituality and general problems or concerns.

When you seek the counsel of the runes, these will probably comprise the bulk of your questions. Concern for the immediate is only natural. It is those day-to-day questions of living, working and loving that can fill your mind at any given moment. It is helpful to have something that can give you guidance, whether your current problems are petty or life-changing.

When people find out you are working with an oracle, curiosity often gets the better of them.

They, too, want the guidance and the illumination the runes can provide. Don't be surprised if you get several requests for divination.

As before, you can decide how detailed you want the answers to be. Using fewer stones means a more general reading, while using more stones gives a more targeted answer. For the casual question of an acquaintance, a simple layout might suffice. It will give this person something to look at in his or her life, and won't tax your time or abilities. But you might desire a far more detailed look into your own problems, influences, obstacles and strengths.

In this section, I will introduce you to more layouts, and will use more sample questions to help you familiarize yourself with rune interpretation.

Two-stone reading:
'WHAT IS MY LESSON TODAY?'

You could answer a question like this with a one-stone reading, getting a simple overview of the day, but you might want a little more information than that. Life lessons are composed of both positive and negative energy. You exalt in the positives and should learn from the negatives. These two poles are represented by day and night, light and dark, positive and negative. This layout is different from most, because the orientation of the stone won't necessarily remain as you have drawn it.

Using the question 'What is my lesson today?', pull two stones, placing the first on the left and the second on the right. Pay close attention to their orientation.

1 day:
Upright Raido

2 night:
Upright Fehu

Life lessons are composed of both positive and negative energy. You exalt in the positives and should learn from the negatives.

Arthur has drawn an upright Raido in the day position and an upright Fehu in the night position. Raido then represents the positive influences and the upright Fehu represents the negative. 'What is negative about an upright Fehu?' asks Arthur. This is where this layout differs from others. The day position should hold a positive stone, and the night position should hold a negative stone. Arthur flips the rune in the night position, so that it becomes a reversed Fehu.

Now he has an upright rune in the positive position and a reversed rune in the negative position. However, there must have been a reason that Fehu was drawn upright. This needs to be acknowledged. Therefore, in Arthur's reading, the day rune will have a stronger influence than the night when he interprets the stones.

The same logic applies had he pulled a reversed rune in the positive position (upend the reversed rune and give it less weight). If both are opposite, reverse them and treat them with equal weight. If both land correctly, treat them equally. If he had drawn a stone that had no reverse, such as Gebo, Sowilo or Isa, he could either put it back and draw again, or interpret it as his intuition told him.

In Arthur's current reading, the upright Raido in the stronger, positive position is a rune of travel and movement. He needs to be aware of communication (telephone, email or letters) and any travelling he might do that day. Even a short trip could be significant if he is observant. Because Raido predicts heightened skills of communication and negotiation, it would also be an excellent day for Arthur to clear up misunderstandings or talk business.

What are the negative influences? The reversed Fehu warns of financial loss and delays. But because the stronger influence of Raido alleviates some of the warnings found in a reversed Fehu, Arthur should be able to avoid the more dangerous traps. For example, if he discusses business, he needs to pay close attention to the financial details. If there is a misunderstanding, he should look for the deeper issues and deal directly with them, instead of the surface complaints. With only two stones, Arthur has found some solid advice, has put some possible dangers in the spotlight and has the tools to deal with any surprises.

EXPLORING YOUR FUTURE

Can runes predict the future? No. The runes can forecast a possible future, but primarily the runes are a means of bringing to light those issues and influences you need to be aware of in order to bring about positive changes. The future is yours to shape. That said, whenever someone uses a divinatory source, the thought 'What will the future bring?' remains. After all, if you could accurately predict the future, you would be able to avoid pitfalls and traps, take advantage of opportunities and guide your life towards goals with a fair degree of certainty. You would also know to be out of the house when your in-laws decide to pay a spontaneous visit.

The way to prepare for the future is to learn from your past and to guide your present. The runes are not tied to time.

You can ask about your past, present and future, and you will receive guidance. You can ask about yourself or a friend. Your questions can be very precise or general. You can draw a single stone or a dozen. What your runes can tell you is limited only by your imagination and the time you spend with them.

In this section, I will introduce you to some more layouts, and the questions that we ask of the runes will be focused on the future. There is no need to use a crystal ball if you have the runes.

Two-stone reading:

'WHERE WILL I BE IN A YEARS TIME?'

Sometimes it helps to get a quick overview of where you might be heading. Will your life be the same in a year's time as it is today? If you continue on your current path, where will it lead? To get an answer, you can use a modified three-stone reading.

In this layout, the 'today' rune is what is going on in your current life. The middle stone outlines the challenges you will meet and the final stone is the result (in one year's time), if you meet these challenges.

1 today:
reversed
Mannaz

2 challenges:
upright
Berkana

3 one year:
Inguz

Using runes for positive change **125**

SAMPLE READING:
reversed Mannaz, upright Berkana, Inguz

While doing a reading for Tim, I drew a reversed Mannaz in the today position. This rune warns that he is standing alone and may have an enemy. It also indicates the possibility of someone foreign entering his life.

Happily, things improve immediately with an upright Berkana in the challenges position. This rune of family, fertility and intuition shows a strong path out of the suspicion and loneliness of the reversed Mannaz. Tim needs to fill his life with people he can trust, such as family members or friends who are as close as family. There

is a sense of rebirth with Berkana and this could mean that to escape his current problems, he needs to look at making some changes. A new line of work, a new female companion or perhaps a new attitude towards his own life might help Tim escape from the dark times he is currently experiencing.

This interpretation is heavily reinforced by the cyclical rune, Inguz, landing in the result position. It also speaks of a new beginning and assures fruitful success if Tim is willing to do the work. By divesting himself of the negative forces in his current life, Tim will be challenged to start anew. If he does so, by this time next year he will reap the rewards.

CONCLUSION

You now have all the tools you need to understand the runes. If you are faced with a difficult decision, feel unsure of yourself or the direction in which you are going or just want to have a little fun, you can call on the runes. As long as you remember that they are just a guide, you should have a long and healthy relationship with them.

Here's hoping that your life is filled with Wunjo!

You now have all the tools you need to understand the runes.